T0418188

On the Beach

Written by Emily Bone

Illustrated by Cinzia Battistel

Designed by Anna Gould

Seashore consultant: Zoë Simmons
Reading consultant: Alison Kelly

Contents

Life on the beach

A beach is where land meets the sea.
Lots of animals and plants live on the
beach and in the surrounding water.

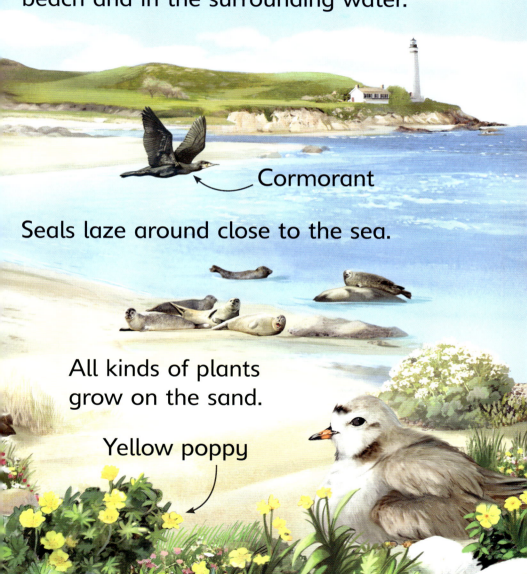

Cormorant

Seals laze around close to the sea.

All kinds of plants
grow on the sand.

Yellow poppy

Tides

Sometimes the sea covers a beach and at other times the beach is bare.

When it's completely covered, like this, it's called high tide.

Gulls can float on the water.

When the beach looks like this, it's called low tide.

Birds hunt sea creatures on the sand.

Oystercatchers

Clam

5

Rocky pools

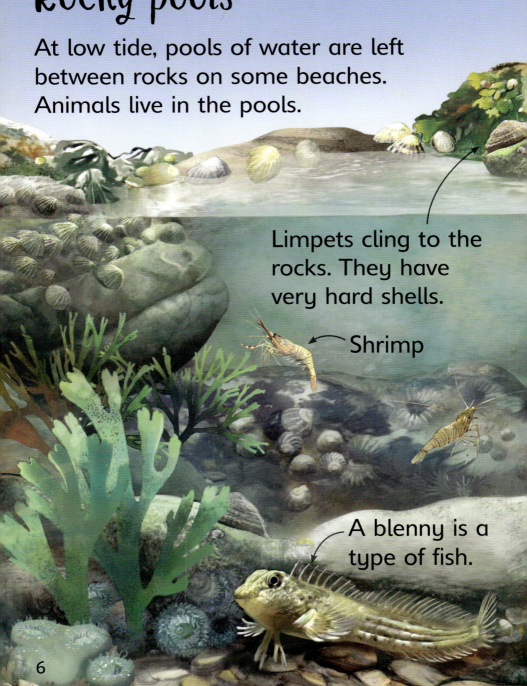

At low tide, pools of water are left between rocks on some beaches. Animals live in the pools.

Limpets cling to the rocks. They have very hard shells.

Shrimp

A blenny is a type of fish.

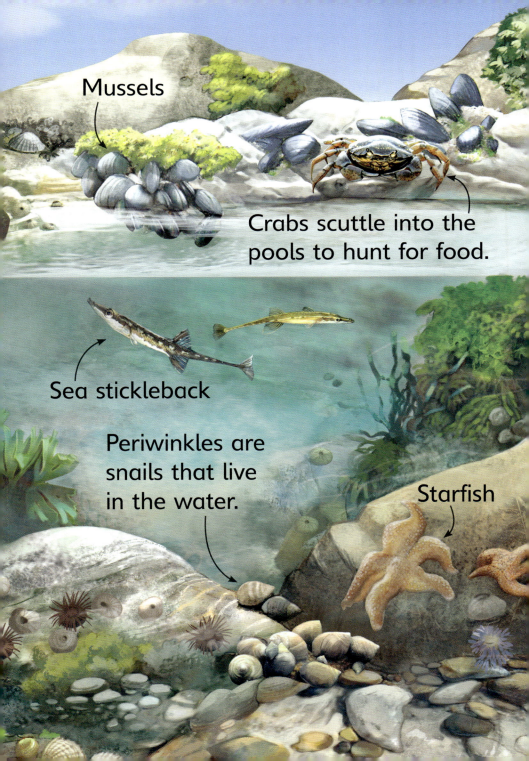

Mussels

Crabs scuttle into the pools to hunt for food.

Sea stickleback

Periwinkles are snails that live in the water.

Starfish

Tough shells

Some of the creatures that live in these pools have hard shells. This protects their soft bodies inside.

Barnacles attach themselves to rocks. They stick out their legs to catch food.

Cowry snails live on the rocky floor of the pool.

Hermit crabs don't have shells.

They look for old shells left
behind by other sea creatures.
Then they crawl inside.

Beach plants

It can be very windy and wet on beaches. The plants that grow on them have to be tough to survive.

Beachgrass has thick, strong leaves.

The leaves and flowers of sea holly are tough and spiky.

Seaweed grows in the sea. It stays slimy and wet when it washes up on the beach.

Thrift grows in the gaps between rocks.

Shallow seas

Many animals live in the shallow seas surrounding beaches.

Sealions swim around hunting for food.

Porcupinefish are covered in sharp spikes. They puff up if they're attacked.

Sea anemones have stinging tentacles to kill and catch animals to eat.

Sea urchins cling to rocks. They have long spikes on their bodies.

Beach birds

Lots of birds live on beaches and hunt for food in the sea.

Pelicans dive under the water and scoop up fish in their beaks.

Other birds find food on the beach.

Redshanks have long beaks to pull creatures out of the sand.

Turnstones look under stones and seaweed for food.

Puffins

Puffins are birds that make nests on the cliffs next to some beaches.

They use their feet and beaks to dig a burrow in soft ground.

The mother lays an egg in the burrow. She sits on the egg to keep it warm.

A chick hatches out of the egg.

The parents hunt for fish and bring them back to feed the chick.

The chick grows bigger. After around a month, it leaves the burrow.

Sea otters

Sea otters find food in the waters around a beach.

They dive down to pick up sea creatures, such as clams.

They collect rocks too.

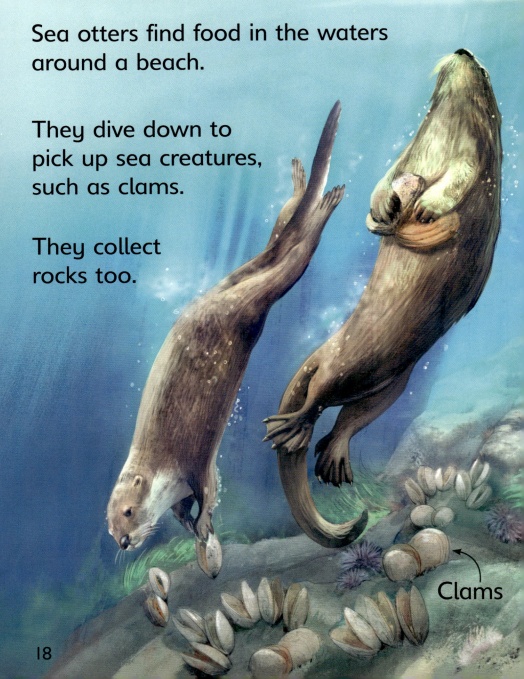

Clams

An otter floats on its back and lays a rock on its tummy.

It hits a clam on the rock until the shell breaks open.

Then it pulls out the soft insides of the clam and eats them.

Cold beaches

Some beaches are very, very cold.
They can be covered in snow and ice.

Weddell seals live in Antarctica.
They rest on the icy shores.

Their thick, fat bodies
keep them warm.

Penguins dive into
the freezing cold
sea to hunt food.

Adélie
penguin

Their feathers are covered in oil.
This keeps the cold water away
from their skin.

Antarctic
silverfish

Warm shores

Other beaches are very hot. Lots of creatures live in the warm, shallow sea next to the beach.

Parrotfish

Seahorse

Coral is a type of animal. It clings onto rocks.

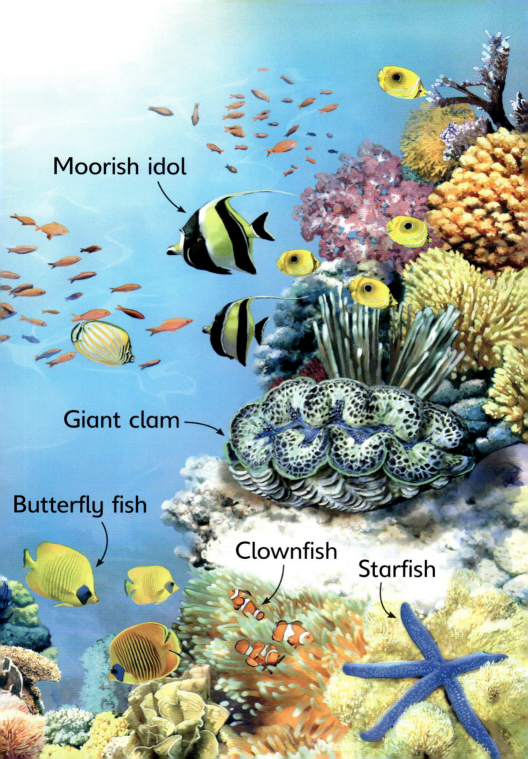

Moorish idol

Giant clam

Butterfly fish

Clownfish

Starfish

Sea turtles

Sea turtles live in warm seas. They use their big flippers to swim through the water.

Jellyfish

These hawksbill sea turtles are hunting sea creatures.

Sea sponge

Turtles come onto beaches when they're ready to lay eggs.

They dig a hole in the sand and lay eggs inside it. Then they bury them.

Baby turtles hatch out. They dig their way to the surface and then crawl back to the sea.

On the sand

Some creatures live on or under the sand on a beach.

Lugworms dig under the beach. They leave piles of sand on top as they go.

Ghost crabs live in burrows. They come out to catch food at night.

A mudskipper is an unusual type of fish that can live on the sand and in the sea.

It uses its strong fins to crawl across the sand...

...and swim when it's in water.

Stormy beach

Sometimes there are storms. These can make beaches very dangerous.

Strong winds make huge waves that crash onto the beach.

The sea is calm after a storm. Lots of things have been washed onto the sand.

Mussel shells

Cuttlefish bone

Heart urchin shell

Blue jellyfish

Glossary

Here are some of the words in this book you might not know. This page tells you what they mean.

 high tide - when the sea is completely covering a beach.

 low tide - when a beach is bare and no longer covered by the sea.

 seaweed - a plant that lives in the sea. It can survive out of water too.

 tentacles - long, thin parts of a sea creature. Some tentacles can sting.

 coral - tiny animals that cling to rocks. They live in warm seas.

 flippers - wide, flat arms or legs used by sea animals for swimming.

 fins - thin, flat parts of a fish's body used for moving through the water.

Usborne Quicklinks

Would you like to discover more about beaches and the things that live there? You can visit Usborne Quicklinks for links to exciting websites with videos, amazing facts and ideas for fun things to make and do.

Go to **usborne.com/Quicklinks** and type in the keywords **"beginners on a beach"**. Make sure you ask a grown-up before going online.

Notes for grown-ups

Please read the internet safety guidelines at Usborne Quicklinks with your child. Children should be supervised online. The websites are regularly reviewed and the links at Usborne Quicklinks are updated. However, Usborne Publishing is not responsible and does not accept liability for the content or availability of any website other than its own.

Nautiluses are creatures that live in shallow seas next to beaches. They use their tentacles to grab food.

Index

Acknowledgements

Managing Designer: Zoe Wray

Additional design by Hannah Ahmed

Digital retouching by John Russell